# SECRETS TO SUSTAINABLE LIVING

*On the Road to a Zero Waste Lifestyle, From Recycling/Reusing, To Growing Your Own, To Composting, and Even Backyard Homestead*

# Introduction

Sustainable living is a practice that is based on the premise that the quality of life can be maintained while sustaining the number of people using the planet's natural resources at a level where the resource can be replenished. It involves adherence to the Principle of Minimum to sustain the earth's biodiversity as well as the inherent biological systems that support the earth.

It is important to understand that there is such a thing as reusable resources. As such, sustainable living is not just confined to the use of renewable resources, but it also involves the reuse and recycling of reusable materials. It is important to explore the lifestyle thoroughly to provide answers to questions such as: What can be reused and recycled? Can all materials be reduced to reusable or recyclable form? What are the least toxic materials used in building, manufacturing, and product design?

Sustainable living is a lifestyle that focuses on the quality of life as a whole. It is based on the idea that humans are not sole agents of the planet. Rather, we are dependent on it. Thus, sustainability is necessary to underpin a truly healthy lifestyle while simultaneously protecting the environment and the planet from the depletion and degradation that is resulting from the depletion of natural resources and the accumulation of garbage.

This lifestyle is based on energy conservation and the efficient and frugal use of materials. This is done by avoiding wastefulness and excessive consumerism. As such, the sustainable lifestyle eschews the conventional practices in which resources are used and then thrown away. Indeed, this is the very premise of sustainable living. As such, sustainable living paradoxically espouses the use of renewable resources. These are materials that will never become depleted. As such, they can be used continually.

The conventional, fatalistic view is that the resources in the earth will eventually be depleted. Thus, our living spaces will have to be made from non-renewable resources such as concrete and steel. Sustainable living, on the contrary, promotes the use of renewable resources.

Renewable resources are naturally occurring resources that are replenished over time. They include sunlight, water, land, plant biomass, and fossil fuels. As such, they can be used indefinitely. The solar energy that reaches the earth is used to power the earth. It is estimated that there is more solar energy that reaches the earth in a single hour than is used by all civilizations in a year. Also, the water cycle is a renewable resource. This is because water can be used for both drinking and agricultural activities. Furthermore, healthy ecosystems can be maintained by using renewable resources. This sets food production free from the risk of the consumption of non-renewable resources.

Because renewable resources are only replenished, it follows the notion that sustainable living involves the use of the least toxic materials. As such, materials that are non-toxic, and are degrade-resistant are used, as they do not require extensive formal and material safety, as well as are indestructible in nature.

Sustainable living is a lifestyle that seeks to live in harmony with nature. As such, human interaction with nature must be in harmony with the natural world. There are eight simple things that can help achieve this. The first is sustainability. This means that resource availability results from the efficient and equitable use of existing resources. It also means that humans are not in control of an infinite supply of resources, but rather they are dependent on the resource cycle, where the lifecycle of materials is not interrupted for some reasons.

Secondly, sustainable living is dependent on equity in access to services and resources. This means that everybody is entitled to the services and resources that sustain the environment. As such, the wealth of the few, cannot deprive the poor of those resources.

Another precondition of sustainable living is the sustainable use of technology. This entails that the technology is environmentally friendly, and that the actual use of technology does not pose a risk to the environment.

The final epistemological axiom of sustainable living is the adoption of correct values. This is the realization that human beings are part and parcel of the environment. Thus, respectfully interact with the environment. People must be knowledgeable of the environment and its functions. This entails the adoption of environmental responsibility among human beings. The correct values embrace the culture and collective consciousness of the other.

For sustainable living to be truly implemented, it must be an ongoing process with a continuous and systematic approach. Sustainable living is a complex process which does not happen overnight. As such, it is a continuous process. It must be approached with an all-encompassing approach.

## This book covers:

Zero waste living

How to reuse and recycle plastic products

Sustainable living, growth, and energy

How to invest in the homestead backyard,

And much more...

This book is here to guide you through it all. You will begin this process by learning about sustainable living at large.

## Reasons for living sustainably

• Indigenous communities used a sustainable way of life, by living off the nutrients of the land and the resources surrounding them.

• The risk of a natural disaster can be lessened by using natural resources found in the environment.

• There are just enough natural resources on this earth for the entire population of the world to live sustainably, and not a single resource available for infinite growth.

• It is within human nature to preserve and protect the environment we all live in.

• Anyone can follow the principle of sustainable living if they are willing to give it their best effort.

# Principles of Sustainable Living

Sustainable living strives to become as environmentally responsible as possible. There are many philosophies on the environment, but the most common is the polluter pays principle. Which can be summarized in the following points:

- Reduce, Reuse, Recycle waste

- You should take care of what you take. If you require something, go and get it at the source.

- Waste is a big environmental issue, so if you are not willing to cut down on your waste, you should at least use it properly.

- Composting is a waste-reduction strategy used by many. It does not only preserve the environment, but also helps avoid landfill accumulation.

- Water conservation is a simple way for everyone to conserve the Earth's most precious resource. No matter how little or how large of an attempt you make to help conserve water is going to have a great impact on the environment that we are living in.

- Reduce your carbon footprint. It is possible to cut down on your household's carbon footprint.

- Use energy-efficient light bulbs so that one day in the future we will not need the power plants that are used now because the energy we use today will be the energy we need in the future.

Sustainable living is a commitment that you, as an individual, make to try to make the world better. With that commitment, the world will become better.

There is an inherent correlation between modern society and sustainability.

There are a lot of problems associated with the modern world. Some of these problems are similar to problems that existed for centuries, and some are new problems that were acquired during the modern era.

For example, consider global warming. If one were to look at the glacial ice cores, it is evident that even though the world was a lot colder back then, there was never enough melting to cause the earth to flood the oceans. This is because the world today has less landmass than previously, and the sea levels are also a lot higher than ever before. Both of these are due to large, dense populations inhabiting the coastal areas.

## Goals of sustainable living

Aside from being environmentally friendly, sustainable living can also be used as an educational tool.

• It can be a good way to teach children how to treat the environment more responsibly.

• These lessons are necessary for a lifetime of living.

• By teaching our children the importance of the environment and giving them the incentive and tools to understand the consequences of their actions, not only can they develop a sense of responsibility, but they will also be able to become more aware of the environment around them.

## Towards sustainable life after technology

Sustainable living can be a better alternative for future generations by helping them without destroying the environment.

Life after technology is quite different from a traditional way of life. It is a much more challenging world in many ways. Due to the many scientific and technological discoveries, the traditional approach to living will have to be adjusted for the current times. The main goal of the future is to preserve and protect the environment and it will, in turn, hopefully preserve the natural resources.

The goal is to maintain the earth as a healthy balanced environment to ensure the continuous existence of humanity, and to keep humanity sustainable for future generations.

## The means of sustainable living

There are many ways to promote sustainable living. The first way to influence sustainable living is by starting a new business.

- Small businesses are a way to get financially sustainable.

- There are many businesses which can help get the resources needed.

- By conducting experiments with new products, business stakeholders or small manufacturers can help reduce the pollution of the environment.

## Sustainable growth

Sustainable growth is a strategy for making the current and future economies of a country more robust and secure. It deals with being able to satisfy the wants and needs of the people without being detrimental to the environment.

Sustainable growth is the process of reformulating the priorities in such a way that economic growth is accompanied by a steady rise in the level and living standards of the people of the world.

## Sustainable energy

Sustainable energy is the term used for the energy that is created from renewable energy resources. Examples of these natural energy sources include the sun, water, and wind. These resources are naturally renewed, and they do not cause any form of pollution after their use and are often referred to as green energy. Green energy is the energy that is obtained from the renewable resources of the world. The main difference between green energy and conventional energy is the way the energy is produced. In the case of green energy, the technologies used are renewable as they produce zero or few harmful greenhouse gases or other pollutants. It only uses naturally occurring renewable resources to produce energy. In the case of conventional energy, the technology used does not use the natural occurring renewable resources, rather it uses non-renewable resources which has more harmful consequences to the environment.

# Chapter 1. Eat More, Throw less: No Waste Kitchen

For most people around the world, eating out is a common habit. Many people spend a great deal of time and money on eating out. With changing times, people are moving towards a zero-waste approach in their everyday life. One aspect of the zero-waste approach is to eat at home and avoid food packaging waste, including the food packaging waste from eating out at restaurants. Throughout this chapter we shall look at how to save on food packaging waste by eating at home and shopping in bulk.

Sustainable living combines activities of *living efficiently* and *living with less* to create an environmentally sound life. The primary goal of sustainable living is to protect the environment for future generations, by inspiring people to find new means and methods to create a healthier environment. Sustainable living also requires people to protect the environment. Today, sustainable living is practiced by millions of people from all walks of life. It is a growing trend that many people are working towards to minimize their impact on the environment.

The problem with eating at restaurants all the time is that food packing waste increases. Most of the restaurants use large cardboard or plastic food packing for their food orders. What does more food packaging mean? It means more energy usage, more water usage, more toxic chemicals, more garbage, and more landfill. An increase in all these resources means more greenhouse gases. Greenhouse gases lead to climate change, climate change leads to global warming and the bleaching of coral reefs, and in turn, global warming leads to global disasters. But what can be done about this?

## How to eat at home and neutralize food packaging waste:

• Preparing food and eat at home.

• Eat smaller amounts of food because it requires less packaging.

- Avoid purchasing items that use food packaging, e.g., frozen food, frozen pot pies, burrito bowls.

- Avoid mass-produced items like frozen meals.

- Avoid fast-food chains.

- Avoid restaurant chains.

- Avoid packaged goods like canned meats, canned vegetables, and canned soups.

- Avoid restaurant dishes like tossed salads.

- Avoid buying drinks.

- Save water.

To minimize water, use at home, consider using alternative methods, such as hand-washing dishes instead of using dishwashers. In some cases, installing water-saving devices can also help reduce water usage. To reduce water usage for baths, consider taking short showers instead of baths. When bathing children, be sure to insulate the tub properly, and even consider using waterless hand sanitizers to reduce water usage.

## Buy in smaller amounts and start a zero-waste kitchen.

- Purchase items in smaller quantities.

- Consider shopping at multiple stores to get what you need from a variety of stores instead of purchasing one large item from one store to see if it can be combined with something else in the same store.

- Use composting facilities when available.

- Use waste disposals when available.

- Buy items pre-cut.

- Buy items in bulk.

- Buy in season.

- Buy organic.

- Buy local.

## Reduce food packaging waste by eating at home.

- If we all made a point of avoiding all the single-serve items of food in plastic packaging, we could save the planet.

- If we all made a point of buying produce at the farmer's market, and consuming food before it goes bad, we could save the planet.

## Kitchen rules:

**Rule 1:** Don't buy stuff you don't need. Never buy more than you need.

**Rule 2:** If you're bringing it in, you're putting it out. This is an all-inclusive rule. Any in, any out.

**Rule 3:** Invest in reusable bags. Store them in your freezer. Bring them to the store on your next grocery run. For example, try a lettuce bag instead of putting the lettuce in a plastic bag. If you can't find anything, buy some cheap terry cloth, and make your own.

**Rule 4:** Put it back where it belongs. For food, that's the kitchen or fridge, depending on what it is.

**Rule 5:** If you don't use it all, give it away. People need stuff you don't need anymore.

**Rule 6:** Don't use something more than once. You don't want to have to wash food preparation items more than once.

**Rule 7:** Store it all within reach. Wrap food prep items in freezer paper before putting them in the freezer. Keep them labeled.

### Zero-waste kitchen recommendations:

1. Store stuff you don't use regularly in the freezer. Otherwise, these items could get in the way of things you need to see and use regularly, and those things could get wasted if not seen and used.

2. Use one bin for all your food scraps.

3. Store ripened fruit in the fridge.

4. Use the kitchen sink for washing veggies. Use a food prep pot to clean harvested veggies. Put the pot in the sink, fill with water, add an appropriate amount of bleach, and clean away.

5. Put their leftover food away.

6. Get a dehumidifier and set it in an open cabinet in your kitchen. The goal is to have the dehumidifier suck away moisture from the air to help the kitchen smell fresh. The cooked items of food and fresh produce smell so much better than the air that humans expel and breathe.

7. If you bought food that is still good, chop it up to consumer right away or freeze it. You can use the food in the future, but remember, it might not be the same as the day you bought it.

Sustainable living in the kitchen involves using the kitchen to maintain a zero-waste lifestyle and minimize waste. The kitchen is a critical part of the sustainable living process because most of the efforts required to reduce waste start in this room. Cleaning the kitchen is also a critical step to eliminate germs and reduce odors. These are two key steps toward a sustainable life. It is economical to clean floors and dishes properly because this helps to minimize wasting water. For a zero-waste life, every step is important.

# Chapter 2. Reuse, Recycle: No More Plastic Packaging

Plastic packaging is a big contributor to our waste generation, and single-use products are the worst. Some people would say, "Yes, we have to reduce our packaging waste and plastics" while others would say: "I cannot live without plastic" or" Plastic is fantastic". Let's take a hard look at the facts and understand how we can eliminate the use of plastic.

All the pre-packaged food products in the supermarket are available in plastic containers. This includes meat products, dairy products, fruits & vegetables, processed food, and pretty much everything else you purchase. Is this good news by any chance? NO!

Now let's get into the recycling dilemma. Recycling saves energy and reduces the production of new plastic. Manufacturing plastic from precursors (natural gas is used for making them) takes a lot of energy while recycling plastic back to plastic takes less energy. Recycling keeps the plastic out of the landfills which in turn cause problems with air and water pollution. Plastic recycling is a must and should be easy to do. So why is it so hard?

There are so many plastics used today that it is difficult to recycle all of them. The plastic film both blown and extruded, such as polyethylene, polypropylene, PVC, and LDPE are easiest to recycle.

A major reason is that recycling programs are not available in most places and even if you have them around, they aren't economical. This is especially true for rural areas. So, with all this in mind, let's look at how we can make tough decisions.

If you are on a road trip or a long vacation, you can get some snacks in an air-tight and hard plastic packaging. You can use a glass container for a salad dressing jar. You can also use a bread bag for frozen food rather than a Ziploc bag, or carry snacks and sandwiches in paper bags rather than Ziploc bags. Avoid plastic water bottles and instead use stainless steel water bottles with a filter.

When grocery shopping, plan your meals and buy only what you need. Carrying containers to put items in reduces packaging and waste tremendously. There are so many bulk bins in the supermarket. Most of us don't look around to find these counters, we just grab the packaged in plastic items, as it is much quicker and easier.

Another method of shopping is to go to a farmer's market or a Boho market. You can find some old-fashioned dried foods in these places and they are reusable. Instead of putting dry fruits into a Ziploc bag and throwing it away when you get back home, try using an airtight container instead.

Instead of using plastic sandwich bags, use paper bags to package ingredients for a family meal.

You can do a lot by avoiding the use of plastic and you will find that you are saving a lot of money and resources.

## The importance of recycling and reuse are imperative.

With this initiative, we want to inspire everyone to make a stand to carry on the message of "Zero Waste Living", as the habit of polluting the environment must be eradicated. What motivates your heart to start a zero-waste lifestyle and what are you willing to give up? Give this a little bit of thought.

The biggest problem these days is that plastic gets thrown around like trash and can be found in all corners of the street. Based on the fact there are many different types of plastics, there is no real way of disposing of them. We can use them but what do we do with the discarded plastic items? This can pose a big challenge for all of us. For such a long time, people have been making attempts at recycling and reusing plastic. However, at what cost to the environment? What is the cost to our planet?

Plastic waste presents a big problem as it has various dangerous impacts on the environment, such as for marine life, where plastic waste is the number one threat to these underwater ecosystems. It almost seems impossible to stop plastic waste from generating these widescale issues, as well as getting people to notice these issues, and take action. The biggest problem with plastic waste is that it is highly toxic and can be potentially fatal. There is also a profoundly serious problem with waste plastic litter and debris, all of which is making a huge impact on the environment and putting the ecological systems worldwide under dire threat. According to a study carried out by the National Geographic Society, "plastic bottles and packaging make up 5% of the total waste generated by human society." This type of waste is mostly affecting the world's marine species.

Dumping plastic trash in the ocean is certainly not to be taken lightly. The plastic trash that we produce is so big in bulk that it can come in big waves in the sea and can be very deadly. A surge of plastic trash can kill thousands of animals and cause great damage to the environment of that specific area. There is a team of researchers from the University of California, San Diego, who have discovered that, "20 million tons of plastic waste enters the oceans every year, and that around 80% of the waste never breaks down." Also, the researchers have found "clumps of microscopic plastic fibers called micro plastics" all over the world's oceans. Micro plastics are made of plastic debris and are of a minute size, which can also mean that the big problems posed by plastic waste might just be becoming worse. So, for all of us, to make sure we are doing the right thing in protecting the environment, we need to take action and begin to deal with our plastic waste properly.

Reusing or recycling your plastic wastes is much better. Many organizations that offer programs for recycling waste plastic are helping the cause as we speak. To begin this process, we need to understand what waste plastic is, and what types of plastic we can get rid of.

One of the types of plastic waste we produce is BPA-free plastic bottles. Instead of incinerating this plastic waste, we can safely scrap them or recycle them for energy. While experts are still trying to figure out what exactly is this plastic that makes it such a threat to the aquatic world, we know that high concentrations of this type of plastic can trigger hormonal changes.

Eradicating plastic packaging is important as it assists in zero waste life and creates an eco-healthy lifestyle. All the things that marine life consumes, humans consume too. If human beings don't care for their health and for the planet, then they are often simply putting themselves at risk. Plastic and non-biodegradable products are among the many reasons why the ocean is poisoned, lakes are polluted, and the air is becoming toxic. The main purpose of plastic products is to use the same one repeatedly, but obviously, that is not what happens in reality. Most of these products are not recycled and remain in piles for a long time without decomposing.

Do the basics: take action with a conscience. One significant way to start creating an eco-friendlier world is to buy products that are eco-friendly. Look at the label to check the ingredients and manufacturing process complied. Prevention of more environmental damage is impossible if one does not take the first step to make a change.

Sustainable living is a challenge and certainly not a piece of cake. With that said, it is time to take the environments side, and take action. Very few people in today's society are actively advocating for the protection of our planet. Each one of us has a small role to play in helping the environment, otherwise someday the life that we have created on this planet will not remain alive.

Plastic is a dangerous material that even nature cannot digest. It can take hundreds of years to break down these non-biodegradable products, and lack of awareness and inadequate spread of information are two reasons why the problem of plastic pollution is much worse than what we imagined. There are currently so many things that are harming the environment, but using plastic is one of the most hazardous things. The positive attitude worldwide towards plastic is a big threat to the health of the environment, and many countries are implementing policies to minimize the use of plastic and discourage people from using it.

Environmentalists are trying to save the planet's flora and fauna by banning the use of plastic bags, bottles, and straws. But the bad part is that it is not just businesses that have to reduce the use of plastics, even we are responsible for the environmental threat. In many of our daily routines, we contribute to the damage on the environment due to the use of various plastic products. If we do not change our ways, then severe problems will occur due to the increased usage of plastic products, and these will negatively impact the environment.

Plastic is a material that does not get decomposed rapidly and can take hundreds of years to break down. When we throw these plastic products out, they damage the environment and harm marine life. Even when they are disposed of despite careful management, they can stay in nature for a long time. There are many microorganisms that exist in these plastics, that often enter the human body, as well as the lives of the marine life, so we are often essentially putting our own lives at risk, along with the lives of our underwater ecosystems.

When the plastic waste is in nature, it can get into most herbs or plants. Thus, for the organisms that humans feed on, consuming plastic material can be a problem. The best example of this problem is with our fish. Fish are often the ones that eat the plastics thrown in the ocean, and then choke to death.

Plastic is made up of several different types of chemicals, depending on the type of plastic used in the production process. The most common chemical that is used in almost every type of plastic is Phthalates. Unfortunately, these chemicals are extremely damaging to the environment and can even be dangerous for the human body. Phthalates coat the plastic and make it a perfect insulator. So, the plastic stays longer in the environment, and the concentration of these chemicals can increase. Many chemical companies are creating new plastic compounds that contain no phthalates. And phthalates are already banned in several countries, but these new plastic compounds are also harmful to animals and humans. It is exceedingly difficult to tolerate phthalates and therefore, we should try to avoid them.

Acetaldehyde is another hazardous chemical that is produced by the plastic with the help of Phthalates. Recycling these plastic products can create very harmful chemical reactions and could be extremely dangerous for the environment. The main reason for this is that these new compounds melt at a lower temperature than previous plastics. It should be noted that these products can even melt in our hands.

Another chemical, called Bisphenol A (BPA) is also used by the plastic industry. It is a toxic chemical that can be found in things like plastic bottles, plastic containers, and other similar products. This chemical can be passed to the human body when we consume liquids, or even when we consume foods that are stored in BPA containers. Some countries have regulated the use of this chemical, but many countries still allow these.

Pesticides are mostly used in the agriculture area. The chemical kills the insects that eat the crops. It is very harmful to the environment and the use of pesticides can increase microorganism pollution.

Even our day-to-day plastic products are causing a lot of harm to the environment. It takes decades for the plastic to degrade and smaller parts of plastic will break off and float in the ocean. Therefore, we must reuse and recycle any kind of material, and we should try to avoid single-use polyethylene plastic bags.

Furthermore, the manufacturers of plastic straws should stop making straws that are too small or use plastic straws that can be recycled. Some types of plastic such as PET can be recycled, but some types are not recyclable. The plastics industry should rather focus on making plastic products that can be recycled easily.

Using plastic products puts our environment and lives at risk, because of the harmful chemicals that can enter the human body. It can cause serious problems for the environment and our marine lives. To reduce the use of plastic products, governments, schools, and NGOs can create awareness among the public. The government can also try to help NGOs in creating awareness on various issues such as plastic products and recycling. It is also important for us to stay away from purchasing products like plastic bottles, and when we buy plastic products, it is important that we take care of the environment when throwing them away. We could use recyclable products and recycle all the other common products. The plastics industry should try to make more recyclable plastics.

Now that we understand exactly what is harming the environment, we need to make sure all of us are warned to stop using such plastics. Only then would we be saving the various marine species that are in great danger and we would realize that everything we do is not just for us, but also for the safety of our planet. So, let us all join hands to reduce our plastic waste and take care of the environment.

# Chapter 3 Raising Food - Grow vegetables at Home

Growing vegetable at home or in a backyard helps with sustainable living as well as with food security. A garden full of vegetables is a kitchen full of good cooking. Vegetables are rising in popularity on the internet. Growing vegetables is on-trend in the alternative homes business. It has managed to achieve some degree of success, and you can too.

Using sunlight and capturing rainwater is the best way for the sustenance growth of vegetables. Vegetable gardening is a long-term investment. You can impress and surprise family, friends, and neighbors with the results. Food grown in your backyard fills the plate, wallet, and your loved one's hearts. However, vegetable gardening must be done with efficiency. You must apply the right techniques at the right time and have the right tools around to do it right.

Watering the garden is also a critical part of success in growing vegetables. It is common in some parts of the world that the water supply is a limited resource. Finding water for the garden is increasingly becoming a challenge. The modern urban environment is built for warmth and convenience. Backyard vegetable gardening is the antithesis of comfort. Gardeners need to prepare their tools and choosing the right tools will help you accomplish the task with ease.

With the right tools, you can get into vegetable gardening even if you do not have a green thumb. Irrigation tools and watering can create abundance in your backyard. Your efforts will be rewarded with good harvests. Good tools will also help you invest in the organic movement. With good tools, you will have a good chance of improving the soil from the very beginning. The best way to lower the cost of vegetables in your diet is to grow them yourself. You will need to invest a little money up front and throughout the growing process, but this investment will pay for itself quickly as your grocery bill shrinks. The most cost-effective way to have fresh vegetables is to cut out all the middlemen and grow your own.

## Make money with a vegetable garden

We just finished talking about saving money by avoiding the farmer's market, but the flip side to that particular benefit is the fact that you could be the one selling vegetables there. If you have your garden then you can harvest your crops, take what you need for yourself and sell the rest locally. Many gardeners even maintain a garden for themselves and one for crops they are planning to sell.

If you are growing vegetables in your garden anyway, then adding a couple more with the intent to sell what you produce can be a great way to earn back your initial investment. If you switch to eating your vegetables rather than buying them, you are going to save money on the grocery bill, but the initial investment will not be repaid in the strictest definition. If you take those same vegetables and sell them, you can earn back that investment with extra to cover the interest.

Keep in mind that the initial investment to start a vegetable garden is not extremely high anyway, so it can quickly turn a profit if that is your intention. Outdoor gardens will only be able to make money on a seasonal basis, but indoor vegetable gardeners can keep growing vegetables throughout the year. We are going to focus on outdoor gardening here, but indoor growing is worth researching if you intend to use your vegetable gardening skills to earn money.

## You eat healthier and more creatively when you have a vegetable garden

The lack of harmful chemicals is only one of the reasons that having your vegetable garden is a healthy choice. When they start growing their vegetables, most beginners are surprised at how much they can harvest. These nutritious plants end up in all sorts of different meals, if for no other reason than the fact that they need to be used (or preserved) before they can go bad. To boot, these vegetables are free if you already have the supplies, whereas store-bought vegetables cost you money. Due to cost, most people purchase smaller quantities of vegetables compared to what a vegetable garden can yield in a good season.

Let's say you are a fan of carrots, so you purchase them a lot. It is likely that you purchase one or two bags of them in your fridge at any given time. You might consider buying more of them when they are on sale, but then many people find they do not go through them fast enough to get through the bags before the carrots go bad. Since there are only so many carrots in the house, it is always an easier choice to cook them up in a way that is familiar and safe. However, when you have tons of them from a good harvest, you will find yourself getting creative with your meals. There are thousands of new recipes to be found on the internet every day and it is much less risky to ruin a few carrots when you have tons, unlike when you buy them from the store.

This level of creativity is something that you will often hear new gardeners talking about after their first good yield. People do not consider this to be one of the benefits of gardening because it seems detached from the physical work of planting seeds and getting your hands dirty in the soil. But having more vegetables around the house leads to healthier meals with more variety and experimentation. You might just discover your new favorite recipe this way.

## It is better for the environment

One environmental cost that is a direct result of modern farming practices is the number of chemicals that are poisoning the environment. Most of the chemicals used in your food are not poison in a direct manner. That is, you can eat traces of them without getting sick (though there are exceptions to this), but these chemicals are the most harmful to the environment itself; runoff from fields affects the wildlife in the surrounding areas and seeps into nearby bodies of water. Unfortunately, starting your vegetable garden is not going to have a strong impact on this. This is the result of large-scale operations. But switching from store-bought produce to veggies you have produced yourself will keep you from funneling more money into these harmful practices. Less money being funneled into environmentally abusive hands is always a good thing.

Starting your vegetable garden is more impactful in reducing the number of fossil fuels that are burnt as part of your eating. When you go to the grocery store and purchase vegetables, you are also paying for the gas that was required to move that vegetable across the country. By growing your vegetables, you create food without having to burn fossil fuels, which reduces your carbon footprint. If you sell those vegetables locally, then you can reduce the number of vegetables that need to be shipped into your local area, which means that you are also helping to reduce the carbon footprint of your community this way.

If you do not care about the environment as much, then at least consider the fact that the fewer fossil fuels being burned, the less money you are spending to keep you and your family fed. It would have taken a trip to the grocery store to get your vegetables, but since you have a crop of your own you don't need to waste time, or the gas needed to drive there. All it takes is your two hands and legs and a couple of minutes to go grab something from out of the garden.

## Grow a variety of foods

Maintaining your garden is the most important part of having a garden. Anyone can simply plant some seeds and set up a garden, but it takes a dedicated gardener to maintain and keep the garden healthy and flourishing. There are a few things that you need to take into consideration when looking at the general maintenance of your garden. The first area to observe is the distance between your garden, your trees, and other roots. Trees can be a nuisance when building a garden for a couple of reasons. The clearest reason is the shade that trees provide. While the shade that comes from trees is great for us, it is not good for a vegetable garden. Remember that shade does not allow for vegetables to grow due to their need for sunlight. The second area to consider when looking at close trees is the roots.

Roots can spread, and they can spread quickly. You do not want tree roots getting into your garden. You must make sure that your garden is placed at least 10 feet beyond the drip line of local trees that may be nearby. Keep in mind your neighbors' trees as well when looking at this. Now you may not have a choice and the garden that you are going to plant must be located near a tree. If this is the situation you are in, then this will require the need for a barrier to be dug around the garden that you are planting. Digging a barrier will help block the root incursions. What you want to do when digging this barrier is dig a narrow trench that is either deeper than the existing roots or even better, dig the trench to the hard clay. Once this is done, you are going to want to lay a sheet of some kind of heavy material, such as metal to ensure roots will not be able to penetrate through; this will be placed on the edge. After this is done, fill in the trench with whatever barrier material that you chose and make sure that it is even with the soil or right above it.

If you have any plans of adding fruit trees or any other trees in your backyard, make sure you consider this before you plant your garden, as you want to make sure you have enough space between the two. The best plan would be to sit down and draw out a map of your garden with all the trees, plants or ponds your heart desires. This will allow you to gain a better understanding of what you want, as well as where you would want to place all these things in your garden.

Along with making a drawing of the area in question, you also want to keep in mind the wind in your area. Wind can not only damage plants, but it can completely prevent them from growing. Some areas are so windy that the wind will pull the plants right out of the soil! Do not let this happen to you! If you are concerned with the wind in your area, make sure there is a fence or other type of barrier around your garden to shield it from the wind.

Also, look at the land where you want to place your garden. If you are planning on having your garden on a sloped area, you will most likely need to terrace the beds. Making sure the beds are terraced will keep them level and make sure that water is distributed evenly. This will also help prevent erosion from occurring. Making sure that the beds are level is probably the most important aspect of this. If they are uneven, erosion is more likely to occur.

Another area of consideration, once your garden is in place, is regarding the types of future crops you may wish to grow. Make sure you allow space for these plants in your garden. You do not however have to plant them with your initial garden but if you think you will want to plant more vegetables in the future, plan for them ahead of time! When you are creating your garden, you want to identify specific areas for each of your crops! You should always have goals for your garden. While you may start with a small garden, this does not necessarily mean that your garden must remain small. If you wish, you may have a large garden once you make it through a few successful crop growing seasons! Start small and work your way up to a large garden full of beautiful and delicious vegetables!

Sustainable living is attained by learning some basic techniques and ideas and having them done as a way of life. When you become used to living this way you will become efficient at it and need to spend less time on it. I thought it would be a good idea to present ideas to help you learn to get started. The garden is for many a source of food. You must learn to be comfortable raising food, as I believe it is the only way to eat healthily and to eat without hurting the environment. A garden can also help you build a community. It can connect people at the local level as you share the work and reap the benefits. It can raise your awareness by dealing a lot with the earth cycle of the Up and the Down.

You must be ready to invest time. At first, you may have to spend a lot of time, but over time, you will get more efficient at it. Start small and just enjoy it. As you become better at growing things in the soil, you are getting closer to truly being sustainable. If you do this, you can control what you eat and enjoy it more! Growing food is fun and rewarding! Take the time to learn and do this as part of your life.

There are a few basic things we must do to have a healthy garden. We must have rain (don't let it stop raining)! We need good moisture around the time of year when we choose to plant our crops, so that we have healthy plants. Try to plant at the right time. We can water if we need to, as the soil should not be too dry.

One way to receive water is to get it deep in the soil. Soil with a great deal of organic material in it will retain the water better than sandy soil. If you look at healthy forest soil it will have a great deal of organic matter, lots of worms, and life in it. When you turn on your garden hose and spray the ground it will run off like a river. This water must get deep to stay. The better retention you have, the longer the water stays in the soil. You need a balance of all this.

Then, you need to have sunlight. We need to get the plants growing fast in the early part of the season before the real heat sets in. When you are growing you are competing with weeds and grass, and other plants. You need a good start to beat them. If you get the ool weather veggies started in the early spring, then your favorite crops that were planted later will be too late for them to be at their best quality. The later planted items may be productive but they may not reach their full potential.

Peat is particularly good as a straw bed for plants. It will hold up for a long time as it bsorbs moisture and keeps the plant roots moist. Peat is considered organic matter and dds an extra level of organic matter to your soil. It is a good way to provide bedding nder plants. The idea of a compost pile is for you to create a hole filled with stuff from our yard. This hole can be made by digging and creating the pile and covering it with omething like a rubber tarp to hold it in place. You then start collecting items like greens leaves, grass clippings, manure, kitchen scraps, tea bags, eggshells. All these hings combined will start to break down on their weight. Many people are pushing the dea of a compost pile.

There are a few basic principles here. The idea of a "good' compost pile means that it vas made with a good balance of weeds and grass or leaves in the proper ratios. It neans that it was properly turned or mixed or whatever to have good aerobic activity. 'o make a good compost pile this is important. You must include all the basic things we eed to make a soil balanced. The mixture will incorporate most things from the yard nd the garden. It will have food for the soil life. It will incorporate moisture as well as dd topsoil. This is a good idea for first-time composters. It is also important to make ure you do not make the pile more than a foot or two deep. You do not need all that eight. You also want to be certain you do not put down anything poisonous like erbicides or pesticides or any of those things that will kill the soil life. We will not olerate any chemicals or poisons in the food we eat!

'ood grown in the soil is a miracle to your body, your heart, and your mind. We require ome of these things to stay alive and well. The food garden is the Bible! The Bible says o eat the food grown in the garden. Now that you have a vision of beautiful and elicious vegetables in your garden, you must protect them from getting a disease. 'lants are often very susceptible to diseases. We often find ourselves trying to figure out ow and why our plants got a disease but unfortunately it happens very often. It is nportant to understand how and why our plants get diseases, that way we can do everything in our power to ensure that they are disease-free and that they do not die. There is nothing worse than getting excited about your garden, planting your crops, and then having all your crops die before they even produce anything. When trying to understand plant diseases, you must first be able to understand the disease triangle. The disease can only occur when you have a plant that can get sick, you have a fungus, virus, or another type of pathogen that can attack your crop, and when conditions in the environment such as drought occur. When three of these things happen at once, our plants are at risk of getting a disease.

Now there are things that you can do to protect your plants from getting a disease. The first thing you can do is inspect every single plant before you buy it. Educate yourself ahead of time on what an unhealthy plant looks like. Stores may be selling unhealthy plants and not even realize it. It is up to you to do the research and be able to see for yourself whether a plant is healthy or if it is unhealthy, and whether or not it will be susceptible to disease. Educate yourself by looking up pictures of healthy plants, looking up images, reading on healthy plants, or you can ask for a store clerk to help you with this process as well if needed. Remember, you should always examine everything before you buy it and that includes plants as well. Try looking up the exact vegetable plants that you want to grow and look up healthy pictures of these plants, that way you know what you are looking for! Make sure you never take home a plant with insects, spots on the leaves, or a plant that has unhealthy roots. If plants like these are planted with your healthy plants, you are putting your healthy plants at risk of getting a disease. Once your plants become plagued with disease, it is often exceedingly difficult to get rid of. Remember that and use caution when purchasing plants. You do not want to ruin your entire garden simply by purchasing unhealthy plants because you were unaware of what a healthy plant looks like!

All good things come to those who wait. All gardeners must remember this, no matter how big or small your garden is. We, as humans, love instant gratification. The fun part about gardening is the fact that you get to watch your crops go from nothing to edible vegetables. This process, while it may require patience, is wonderful to see. Remember that when you start planting crops, you are not going to be able to go outside the following day and find your vegetables fully grown and ready to eat. Enjoy the waiting process. This is not only a good practice for you as an adult, but it is good to introduce this to children as well. Gardening involves so many learning lessons for children and patience is one of them. Children, like adults, must learn to be patient and wait for things in life. Nothing will happen overnight no matter how much you want it to. The more time you put into something and the more time you wait for something the better it will be. Use this opportunity to have your child take pictures of the growing plants, now and then, so he/she can compare pictures. Your child will then be able to compare the growth of the plants, from the time you started growing them, to the time when they are ready to eat. This may even be his/her following science fair project! Other lessons about agriculture can be incorporated into this process as well. For example, this is a great opportunity to teach your child about science and biology.

Teach your child about erosion and other areas involved in gardening. If you are not sure about this topic, try buying a gardening guide and read it together. This is a great team project, and you can incorporate many areas of learning into the gardening process as well. If you buy a gardening guide, you will also be able to visually see what plants are supposed to look like, and while yes, your plants may look a bit different, they should look similar. If you do not have anything to compare your plants to, then it will be difficult to see whether you are doing something right. You may start growing pumpkins and when you see flowers developing you may question yourself as to whether you planted pumpkins or flowers. The more you read about the crops you are planting the more knowledge you will gain on each one and you will then know what to look for. That being said, if you read a guide on growing pumpkins, you will then know that when flowers develop on the pumpkin vine, you will understand that this is simply the first stage of the pumpkin growing process! We should all be open to learning more about things in life and gardening is one way to educate ourselves about the world around us.

We often go our whole lives and never understand how things grow or how things work. Gardening can not only teach us a great deal about crop growing, but it can also teach us about ourselves. We may find that we become impatient when our plants are not growing fast enough, or we may find that we completely neglect our plants and leave our initial project to die. Either way, learning different things about yourself is important. If you find yourself being impatient, take this as an opportunity to practice patience, if you

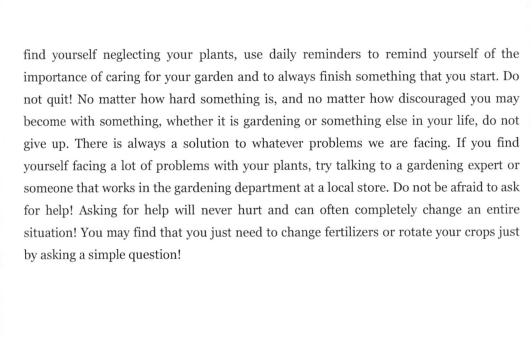

find yourself neglecting your plants, use daily reminders to remind yourself of the importance of caring for your garden and to always finish something that you start. Do not quit! No matter how hard something is, and no matter how discouraged you may become with something, whether it is gardening or something else in your life, do not give up. There is always a solution to whatever problems we are facing. If you find yourself facing a lot of problems with your plants, try talking to a gardening expert or someone that works in the gardening department at a local store. Do not be afraid to ask for help! Asking for help will never hurt and can often completely change an entire situation! You may find that you just need to change fertilizers or rotate your crops just by asking a simple question!

# Chapter 4 Curing and Smoking Meat to Preserve

Curing and smoking are also useful methods to protect your food from spoilage and can fit in with your busy lifestyle. When foods are kept for long periods, they are likely to be at risk of rotting. It is particularly important to store food in a way that will keep it fresh and undamaged. Food preservation and storage is a practice that keeps your food from spoiling, which protects you from meal planning headaches and sickness.

Curing, when done correctly, can keep food fresh for an exceptionally long time. When foods are dried, frozen, or canned they are set to last for months, if not years, but some foods can be preserved forever by curing. Food that has been cured and smoked is barely decaying and is extremely healthy to eat because it contains little to no mold. If you enjoy your fresh meat, this can be a great way to ensure that it stays fresh for a long period of time.

Before you begin, you should make sure you have all the things you need to properly cure your meat. You will need a large amount of salt, sugar, seasonings, and equipment.

**1. Meat and the room.** You will need a lot of patience and a lot of meats. You will want a variety of meat with different fat contents in them. You can use different meat cuts on different occasions to determine which ones you like best. Do a little research and find out what things you can cure and smoke and what the basic process is. Read recipes and find out what you will need to make them. You will want to make a list of the things you need and where you can get them. You will need to make a lot of things if you want to cure enough goods in a long period of time.

**2. Meat, salt, and sugar.** You start by slicing your meats into thin strips. You can use a meat slicer or just cut them into smaller pieces or uneven pieces.

**3. Brining.** You will want to prepare your salt and sugar mix. Mix your desired amount of salt with the required amount of sugar and then place half of this mixture in an airtight container.

**4. Adding meats.** Add your meat to the container and mix thoroughly. You will want to coat all sides of the meat thoroughly with the salt and sugar mixture.

**5. Curing.** You will want to mix your brine often to keep it from settling and coating only one side of the meat. You will want to add different meats to the mixture to get the full effect of whatever you are curing. You can usually store it in a cool, dark place and it will be ready in a day or less.

**6. Smoking.** When you are bringing your meat, you will want to set your sprinkler to run for a long period, so it has plenty of time to get a good layer of smoke on it. If you would like to add different aromas to your meat, you can add things like spice or fruit peelings. You can also keep your meat plain and simply serve it in the future with a Smokey flavor.

**7. Preparing for consumption.** You will want to make sure your meats are ready before you eat them. Wrap them in a different material to keep them clean and to maintain the smokey flavor. If you like the smokey flavor, you can eat them right out of your container. If you do not, keep the meats wrapped until you are ready to consume everything.

Curing and smoking are beneficial in sustainable living and are a helpful way in getting the best out of the meat you have. It keeps you from running to the grocery stores for meat, makes your meat tasty, and helps in food preservation. You do not have to worry about it spoiling, you can leave it out on the counter for a few hours and it will not spoil.

Curing and smoking are amazingly effective to keep harmful bacteria away. It is also used in many other industrial applications. There are multiple methods to protect your food from spoilage and can fit in with your busy lifestyle. When foods are kept for long periods, they are likely to be at risk of rotting. It is especially important to store food in a way that will keep it fresh and undamaged.

# Importance of smoking meat

One of the most important functions that smoking meat and fish plays is that of preserving the food for a longer period of time. Eating fresh food is always good and is healthier than preserved food. However, there are cases where you might not be able to get fresh food or you live in a place where the transport of fresh food is just not possible.

Meats like fish and meat that are taken from domesticated animals, are prone to getting spoilt after a short period of time since they are tainted with bacteria that can spoil the meat and are attacked by several parasitic insects like worms and ticks. To keep the meat fresh and healthy, the curing process is followed.

Curing, or the meat curing process, is the process that stabilizes the meat content with the help of chemicals like salt, nitrate or nitrite, sugar, and spices and keeps the food in preserved form and ready to eat for several days.

In addition to this, there are some methods of meat curing processes that are dependent on the weather and time. Meat can be cured using different methods and some methods of curing meat used at a different time of the year are described below:

**Curing meat during spring:** if you have a lot of meat that you need to preserve for a longer time, you can start curing meat during the spring. The process can be started when the daytime starts increasing and nighttime starts decreasing. This is the time when the temperature is just about perfect to cure meat since the temperature is above freezing and below 40 degrees Celsius at the time. You must prepare the meat by soaking it in a water-rich solution of salt and sugar for a few days. The next step is to rub the meat with the mixture that is made with pure salt, sugar, and spices.

**Prepare the meat for the smoking process now.** If you want to preserve the meat for a longer time, smoke the meat with some heat that will not be over 40 degrees Celsius once the meat is already cured and prepared. The humidity present in the meat is ideally low, which can be achieved by storing the meat in a sealed container above the ground. The meat will not keep as dry if it is stored in the air.

**Curing meat during summer:** the curing process for summer starts after the spring season and you get to start curing meat as soon as the sun makes its appearance in the

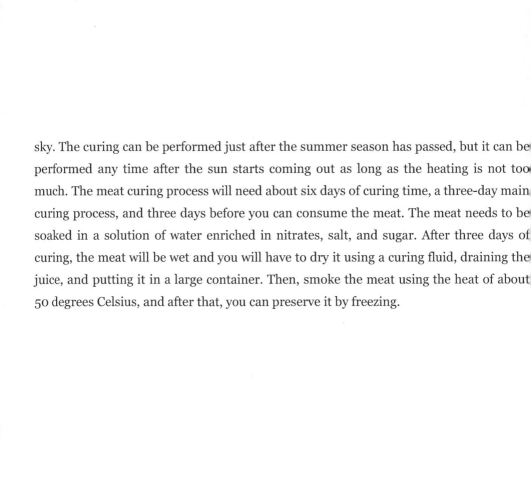

sky. The curing can be performed just after the summer season has passed, but it can be performed any time after the sun starts coming out as long as the heating is not too much. The meat curing process will need about six days of curing time, a three-day main curing process, and three days before you can consume the meat. The meat needs to be soaked in a solution of water enriched in nitrates, salt, and sugar. After three days of curing, the meat will be wet and you will have to dry it using a curing fluid, draining the juice, and putting it in a large container. Then, smoke the meat using the heat of about 50 degrees Celsius, and after that, you can preserve it by freezing.

# Chapter 5 Composting in Your Backyard Garden

Composting helps in sustainable living or zero waste lifestyle by keeping your means of disposing of organic materials at home. You can get rid of odors, weed seeds, and reduce waste by using or composting your kitchen scraps and yard waste. A compost pile takes some time to break down into nutrient-rich compost. You need to manage your compost so that it does not get too hot or too wet. To make compost, you need to add organic material to it. This represents food waste and green waste. You also need to add microbes that will aid in breaking down the material.

## Why You Should Compost

It is good to compost in your backyard since it is beneficial for plants as it adds nutrients to the soil (a major source of food and particularly important for plants). By adding compost to your garden, the nutrients in your garden can be improved. Hence composting in your backyard is more important than you are aware of.

What is compost? Compost is a mixture of organic waste from organic fertilizers. This mixture of organic waste is the most abundant stock in nature. The most abundant organic fertilizer or reservoir of food for all living things in the world is compost. Plant life needs this food most in times of crisis. In the era of globalization, we have made sure to add our waste to our soil. When we are in crisis, we think of digging up our land and dumping the waste of our fast food and other such foods that we have consumed. This is not healthy or efficient.

Let us explain the idea of composting. Suppose a family has a kitchen waste of vegetables and fruits, and in this kitchen, we have a couple of burners. When we burn these materials, we produce all these organic wastes. After throwing out these organic wastes, one can burn them and stop them from spreading out in the atmosphere. After burning it, we can plant a tree or any other plant and hence, add it to the soil. So, the organic fertilizers are not wasted, and the plants can now be depended upon for their food.

The compost is greatly beneficial to plants because it contains hundreds of nutrients and essential elements that are incredibly good for the growth of plants. Hence, anyone who grows plants, be it to grow vegetables, flowers, or fruits, should compost. Composting can be done simply and scientifically.

## The Best Composting Materials

So, how do you get the most out of your compost? You need to start with the best materials when composting at home. Your kitchen scraps, the remains of your vegetables, meat, etc. can be added to the compost. It is better if they are chopped into small pieces to create good drainage in the pile. When you are adding a lot of vegetables to the pile, you should add carbon-rich materials to balance out the moisture and heat.

## Carbon Rich Materials

Carbon-rich materials include straw, leaves, dry plant stems, old newspapers, and sawdust. You should add some manure to the pile or in the form of a compost starter. This gives more microbes and nourishes plants. It acts as a fertilizer and conditioner.

## When You Should Start a Compost Pile

You can get started right away to start composting. You need to put up a simple compost pile so that you can get rid of food scraps and yard waste. You can create a large compost bin from recycled materials in your backyard. To maintain the health of your compost pile, you should maintain a temperature between 131- and 170-degrees Fahrenheit.

There is no real answer to how often you should turn the compost. You should turn it every time there's enough compost for you to put in your garden, but you can do it once a month if you want to.

You can use a composting thermometer to estimate when you should turn it. The thermometer should read between 160- and 180-degrees Fahrenheit. If you are using a ot of fresh grass clippings, you can put a few heated rocks in the middle of the pile to keep it hot.

It is important to compost your backyard garden waste to reduce household waste so that you can use home compost in your garden. You need to get the most out of your home composting efforts, so it is useful to know how much space you will need to set aside for composting in your garden. Additionally, you need to know how to effectively make compost that is rich enough to improve your garden, and you need to know how to check the progress. By following the procedures in this book, you will be able to properly compost your garden waste.

## How and Where to Compost Garden Waste

There are many different types of backyard garden compost bins in the marketplace. However, the most functional garden compost bins are made from durable plastic. The average plastic garden compost bin is about three feet tall, which makes the composting process much easier to check than traditional compost piles in the backyard. After all, with an open compost pile, you do not have any idea what is going on inside the pile. To effectively manage your materials, it is best to have something that can be easily checked from time to time.

Composting your garden waste is relatively easy. Starting your new compost pile in the fall is an important step in the process since compost needs at least six months to fully rot. In the fall, set your garden waste bin in your backyard and gather as many leaves and garden waste as possible from the previous year's garden.

In the spring, harvest your compost from the bin and use it and your garden waste for your spring garden.

Composting your garden waste is an important part of the garden season. It is one of the best ways to reduce your household waste. Additionally, it can save you money on outdoor trash services because you can compost as much as you care to inside your waste bins. By following the steps below, you will be able to properly compost your garden waste in your backyard garden.

It is particularly important to compost your garden waste in your backyard garden. You will need to rent a compost bin to get started since compost piles in your backyard are not enough to deal with the kitchen waste. You will also need to know how much space your garden waste takes up in the garden so that you can easily maintain your compost bin.

The process of composting your garden waste is simple. You will need to set aside enough space in your backyard garden so that you can easily turn and keep your composting bin maintained. The average space needed to compost your garden waste is two cubic yards. This will vary depending on the size of your home and garden.

## How to make compost

For composting to be done on a small scale, there is certain equipment that is required to help make the compost. Some of the equipment includes; a working table, a food cart, a storage can, a container of water, a mixing area, and a compost bin.

Once you have all this equipment, you must gather the organic waste that you will use to make compost. These are examples of organic waste;

**Food waste** like vegetable peels, corns, and fruits.

**Animal waste;** is bones, blood, eggs.

**House waste;** is paper, leaves, and grass.

**Office waste;** is wrappers, paper rolls, pens, and pencils.

All compost needs a nitrogen and carbon source. Nitrogen is in the form of protein. This is especially important because if these items are not included, the nitrogen will be washed out.

1. Place all the organic materials that you have in a container and add water to the container to dilute the waste. This is so that the waste will be able to be used as a medium to initiate the compost.

2. Mix the waste and water buffer to get a wet and organic medium that will become good compost. The compost is in the form of a paste.

3. Leave this mixture to change overnight. As these are inorganic materials, there are certain dead organisms. These organisms are bacteria, fungus, and worms in the waste. These organisms will start to eat the organic wastes and hence, converting it to organic food that can be used by plants. When left overnight, this will be the compost that you need. By the time it is left for more than six months, the compost will turn into humus. This is a black, earthy compound which is particularly good for plants to be grown in it. A slow system of composting is better than a fast one.

4. The compost that is left from the first step is placed in a storage container and kept for some time, then it is used for the good of the plants.

## Composting Problems

If you are having trouble with your compost pile for a few reasons, you can turn it and add more carbon-rich materials to balance out the pile. The carbon: nitrogen ratio is between 25:1 to 30:1. You should see good results. If you are having problems with your compost pile, you will know it. It will smell like rotten waste, ammonia or even nothing at all. This can happen in any compost pile. If your compost pile is anaerobic (without oxygen) you will get bad odors. If it is cold outside, it may be producing methane gas and the pile will not smell good. If your compost pile gets too hot, decomposition can take place. Typically, low levels of carbon are better.

If you add too much nitrogen, you will get humus (brown material). It will get moldy and your plants may start to die. You should add nitrogen-rich materials to balance out the mixture. You can add wood chips or sawdust. They are ich in nitrogen. You can add ged manure to balance out the mixture.

You can supplement your composting with some fertilizer when the pile gets too hot or not aerated properly. If you have a lot of vegetable scraps and leaf compost, you can add fertilizer before you plant.

## Harvest Your Compost

After a few months, the compost is complete. You should be able to harvest the compost from your pile. You should also add water to your compost. If you cannot smell it, it's ready to use. You can store it for up to six months in a thick plastic storage bin. Make sure you use a heavy-duty plastic container. It should be airtight for storing. If you want, you can use it as an amendment to your soil. You can grow plants and add the compost repeatedly to the soil. You should then spread it all around your yard and areas where you want to grow vegetable gardens. If you do not want to bother to compost, consider hiring someone to do it for you. You can compost-convert some of your kitchen scraps and yard waste into compost.

## Benefits of Composting

1. Composting helps in improving the soil fertility of your garden. When plants are grown in the soil, they produce toxins and carbon dioxide in their body. This process is called respiration. Meanwhile, when we mix compost that is a fertilizer with the soil and put the plant in it, it becomes part of the plant. This results in a healthier plant.

2. The composting of different kinds of organic wastes helps in controlling water and soil erosion.

3. Composting of organic wastes can be done at home and you do not have to buy fertilizer from the market for your gardening.

4. Composting is also helpful in preserving the biosphere of our planet. Good compost will help in increasing the area of the Earth and the biosphere of our planet. This also helps in preserving nature and the environment.

I have mentioned some of the benefits of composting, and benefits that can be drawn from composting. The benefits are varied and diverse. If you compost at home, you can save up to 80% of the cost that you pay for buying fertilizer. I have tried to tell you how to make compost and why composting is required. I have also told you about the benefits of composting. Now it's up to you to decide if you want to learn about this method of composting.

# Chapter 6 Biofuel from Compost

Biofuel is one of the main sources of renewable energy that is emphasized in reducing global warming. Biofuel is an energy that is obtained from renewable resources like the sun, plants, and animals, and so on. It is an efficient, clean source since it does not pollute the environment.

One of the main sources of biofuel is composting, which we talked about above.

## The Bio-Fuel Cycle

The bio-fuel cycle is amazingly simple. You can follow three easy steps to get composting.

First, you must collect all waste that produces material that will be used as compost. Since composting involves plants that decompose, you can also use your plants as a form of compost. Then, you need to shred them just like you would for a compost bin. Be careful, though, compost temperatures are high so make sure that you have gloves handy. Lastly, you stuff it into the container. This material will be placed so it will break down easily. The microbes will also help your process by breaking down the material. Remember that the compost needs air circulation to provide good bacteria and micro-organisms that reduce the material.

After several months of shredding, you can see a pile of biodegradable material that will be transformed into good compost. Make sure that there are no large pieces of seeds, leaves, or fruits in this compost pile so it will be easy for the fungi to further decompose the material.

The compost will be placed in a pile so that it can oxidize the microbes that ask for oxygen. The organic material will turn into moist, black, crumbly stuff that smells like mildew. From here, you must use aerobic biodegradable soil.

Making compost is an amazingly simple thing to do. The most important thing is to shred all organic material. It does not have to solely be fruits, vegetables, and leaves. You can use dead plants, dry leaves, or even dead trees.

Inorganic compost material may cause particles to stick to the soybean plants. So, it is best to avoid using inorganic fertilizers and manure in the compost pile.

## Steps on how to use the biofuel energy

Most organic enthusiasts have concluded that creating and using compost is a great thing to do. There are many wonderful benefits that come from composting, specifically composting helps the environment. Question: what should be in the compost pile? Organics matter. As previously discussed, compost should contain kitchen waste, leaves, and grass clippings as well as all fruit and vegetable scraps.

Also, animal waste is better than human waste. Beef, chicken, eggs, and dairy products, as well as other meats, must never be included in the compost pile. A compost pile must contain allowed materials. If the pile contains unauthorized materials, it will not be a good compost pile. Restrictions on the ingredients are important because it helps achieve an even end product. There should be a variety of different items with which you build the compost pile. To make it more successful, you should incorporate many different items into the pile.

Bugs help break down unwanted organic matter into a less toxic form while also speeding up the composting process. There are several different bugs you can use, but generally speaking, the more types of bugs you can include, the better product you'll get. However, not all bugs are safe for compost. Never add any bugs that have been exposed to any pesticides, otherwise, they will not survive. Once you add the bugs to the compost, you must follow the whole process of composting. Over time, the compost will develop a rich green color. This is an important sign of a successful compost pile.

Adding unwanted materials to a compost pile can be a bad thing because the compost pile will not be able to accept the extra material. Cutting down on the waste you create is the best thing you can do. There are things you can do to reduce your garbage, but you must make sure not to overload your compost pile.

Depending on where you live, and the weather can easily determine when it is time to add materials to the compost pile. In the warmer months, adding new materials to the pile every week or so provides the ideal conditions. In cooler months, it is recommended that you add new materials in the fall. Before adding new material to the compost pile, you need to wait for a couple of weeks to make sure there is enough moisture.

## Compost bin starts with the best ingredients

There are several things to consider when starting a compost pile. You should start with your best ingredients. Smaller items should be included with larger composting materials. Ideally, a compost bin should contain food scraps, fruit and vegetable scraps, plant materials, and leaves. You should not start adding pet waste to the compost pile until the compost pile is ready.

## Use a tool that deals with the scraps

After the best items are taken and put in the compost pile, the materials used to make the compost pile should be divided into smaller sections. Each of these sections should be separated with a piece of cardboard. This allows for oxygen to get to the materials as they break down.

After each piece is separated, it should be covered with a layer of sawdust and some soil. The finished product is ready to be spread on the soil. The right kind of compost will encourage earthworms to come into the compost pile.

## Compost pile quality control

Certain materials cannot go into the compost pile at any point. These materials may include dog food, cardboard, kitty litter, grass clippings, and animal waste of any kind.

## Pruning the garden

Here are the basic ways to prune your yard from the compost pile. The best way to determine whether you should take this step is to take a look at your outside compost pile. At the end of last season, inspect it to see what changes were made to make the most of it. These changes may include replacing or moving certain items to different spaces.

If you cannot create a better compost pile, it may be time to move certain items such as by getting rid of items that are not getting as much exposure to the air as others. You can also get rid of any items that have started to rot. Rotting items can harm other items, such as your plants, which is not healthy and nutritious for your garden.

## Get the right machine for the job

If you want to use an out-of-the-box type style of compost pile, you will not be able to fit the pile without adjusting it. You need to have your compost pile under the right conditions and to handle the materials in a manner that will make the pile work properly.

To ensure you are not creating a problem when you add compost to it, it is best to let it settle before dumping it. This can provide you with a safer result when trying to start a garden later. The items you put into the compost pile will be carefully processed, allowing you to make optimal use of them later in the garden.

## Controlling the moisture

It is important to ensure your compost pile is not very wet. You do not want to put dry compost materials with wet compost materials. This is not good for your compost pile and will not allow for the decomposition of materials to occur properly. When mixing compost materials, they should be close but not crush each other.

If you have any very damp compost materials, you can put a tarp or old piece of cardboard on them. Then, get ready to add only one layer of these materials to the compost pile. If you put too many of these materials, your compost pile may become too moist. Try to avoid this, as it can cause many problems for your compost pile.

## Good Composting Advice

There are three main steps to compressing a compost pile. First, you need to increase the population of microbes which will accelerate the composting process. You will need o mix the shredded organic material that contain the waste, with various biological gents, to allow the microbes to live.

Secondly, you need to mix the organic matter with your microbes so that the microbes an decompose the material. The microbes will also help in the conversion of composted material into fertilizer. They also reduce the chances of spore plants.

Finally, you must make sure that you maintain and manage compost at the right time. Make sure it gets enough air and dryness. When the microbes are close to the surface, he compost will take a while to become fertilized.

## What is the importance of biofuel?

Biofuel is important because it takes human intervention to make it, since it comes from natural products and the process is long and complicated. It is also important because biofuel can be used as an alternative fuel for motor vehicles, electric power generation, and heating fuel.

Below is a list of steps that are involved in the making of biofuel.

. Produce degraded cellulosic biomass

. Cellulosic pretreatment

. Enzymatic hydrolysis

. Fermentation

. Separation

. Separation

. Solvent cleaning

. Acidification

. Hydrodeoxygenation

0. Dehydrogenation

1. Stabilization

12. Reforming

13. Dephosphorylation

14. Glycerol production

15. Ethanol and fatty acid production

16. Nutrient addition

17. Packaging

Biofuel is important because it can be used as an alternative fuel in many ways, such as in the case of motor fuel. Also, it can be used for electricity generation, and it can be used for heating. Another reason that biofuel is important is that it can help to reduce the amount of carbon dioxide in the atmosphere. Furthermore, biofuel can reduce the amount of exhaust that is put into the air, because biofuel can be used just like a fossil fuel.

Another function of biofuel is that it can reduce the amount of carbon dioxide in the atmosphere by taking environmental waste products and producing energy and other important materials.

Biofuel from compost is also especially important because it takes substances that would otherwise be put in a landfill or burned and puts them in a controlled environment where they can be turned into energy and other important materials. Also, if there was a lack of biofuel then there would be a lack of energy. For example, if there is no biofuel then people would not be able to use it to produce electricity, to run motor vehicles, or for other important things.

Biofuel is creating controversy because there are many different arguments for and against how well biofuel works compared to other fuels. For example, some people say that biofuel is a good idea because it can take natural materials and turn them into energy. Also, biofuels can be beneficial because it can be a substitute for fossil fuel. However, other people argue that biofuel may not be as effective as fossil fuel in terms of producing energy, and its price can fluctuate too much, depending on the production.

## Conclusion

The composting process can be a great way to make manure and fertilizer. If you can make compost, you can use it for a variety of purposes. With the proper care, this dirt will be a lot better than if you use conventional fertilizers.

Most importantly, the composting process makes composting a safe way to use organic materials. It involves composting and organics at the same time. These two materials naturally help each other decompose without using chemicals. If you know what to observe, you can make great compost that is also good quality.

# Chapter 7 Foraging for Foods in Your Area

We must learn all the possible ways in which we can teach ourselves self-reliance and sustainability. This involves not only food, water, and shelter but clothing, and fuel. I am not saying you are going to go out into your backyard and find a petroleum reserve and magically have fuel. What I am saying is to learn more about the plants, trees, nuts, and pretty much anything you can hunt. To see what you can do about them even if it is to make charcoal and fire with sticks. I am not saying we should only depend on foraging for wild edible plants, if we cannot find anything in our area, fine, we just need to do this as an option.

It must be noted that any one of these survival methods on its own is no replacement for any other, as they must all work in harmony with each other for complete and total survival. Therefore, I am suggesting that you learn to grow your vegetables and berries: a few trees and bushes for some spices and fruits, learn to fish, learn about edible plants, and of course, preserve them so they last longer.

There are certain fruits, vegetables, and herbs that we can preserve in the most environmentally friendly ways. To preserve these foods, we need to learn how to dry them. And then from there, the knowledge will be in terms of preserving them without spoiling them. Many fruits, berries, nuts have many medicinal uses as well. And again, this involves more than just boiling the ingredients. It requires special preparation techniques and preservation methods. And this is of course more than just boiling and letting it cool. On top of this, you will need the required containers for storing the final product.

There are also other resources on the internet that list a variety of foods that can be found in some of the most common areas. And of course, there are always guides that have been written to help you with some of the information regarding the foods and how best to preserve them.

This is all great information about the local food chain. But if we are trying to survive for long periods then we need to learn how to make local staples that do not share the same fate as the majority of either wild or cultivated crops that may be rare or hard to come by in any given area. This will save our time and effort so we can devote it to other things.

The main focus of our search for local foods is to maintain a steady food source so we are not affected if we are in an area where some of the food is scarce. Now having said that, here are some of the things that you need to keep in mind along the way. Try to focus on knowing the basics of what it takes to produce what you need to survive. It is particularly important to focus on this because you will find yourself having to produce a lot of food.

## Know where it is available

If you have a particular area in mind, it is important to choose a place that has a wide variety of food sources.

## How to put together the basics of a garden

Have you identified areas that can yield different types of fruits, vegetables, and grains? You should be able to put together the basics for a supply to be able to survive for quite a period.

## How to store the foods you grow

You need to be able to preserve what you grow, and this is going to be crucial when times get tough. Keep track of all that you have produced so that your garden will yield as much as possible for as long as possible.

## How to prepare your food

How the food will be prepared determines how long the food will last.

## How to be able to identify edible versus inedible plants, fruit, and seeds

Most survivalists tend to focus this part of their research in terms of wild plants, fruits, and vegetables. Information is also needed when identifying different animals that are edible as well as the parts of an animal that can be consumed by humans as well as animals that should not be consumed.

## Foraging assists

• Accessing local foods

• Providing much-needed nutrition

• Cutting your grocery bill

• Reducing the risk of allergic reactions

• Introducing your family to new tastes

Most people in the United States don't know this because the steps have been hidden from them, but vitamin supplements are derived from natural sources. Vitamins and minerals, when combined with other natural products, can work wonders for your body.

Vitamins can be more effective than drugs when it comes to treating certain conditions. Green tea, for example, can protect against disease, help with weight loss, reduce the risk of certain cancers, aid in digestion, improve the immune system and even reduce the risk of depression.

According to the American Thoracic Society, some herbs used in Chinese and Japanese medicine – including astragalus, ginseng, and ginkgo – can be good supplements, too. Plus, these supplements are often more effective than medication when used alone. But what are these, and how should they be taken to be most effective?

When it comes to supplements and vitamins, look for natural sources and supplements. Make sure to take a good look at the label. If you don't know what you're putting into your body, you don't know what side affects you could be subjecting yourself to.

## Natural Antioxidants

One of the most effective ways to combat free radicals and slow down the aging process is with antioxidants. Antioxidants neutralize free radicals to reduce oxidative stress. This stress causes damage to our bodies and skin, as well as symptomatic disease. Antioxidants, on the other hand, create a healthier state through their repair of damaged cells.

The best natural anti-aging supplement, therefore, contains antioxidants, and these include Resveratrol, CoQ10, brewer's yeast, wheatgrass, grape seed extract, green tea extract, super fruit, and white tea extract. These supplements can cause significant improvements in your beauty and health.

When bridging the gap between beauty and health, antioxidants can also help consumers combat over the counter drugs. Many over the counter medications cause side effects that an antioxidant supplement can combat. This means the daily intake of a supplement can treat the aftereffects of some medications, or even be used to treat the problem itself without the risk of adverse reactions.

## Natural Pain Relief

When it comes to natural forms of pain relief, not only do you avoid the side effects of chemical-based treatments such as medications, but you can also help to reduce inflammation during the healing process. For instance, turmeric milk is a natural remedy for inflammation and pain relief. This immune boost also increases your capacity to fight disease, when combined with cinnamon.

## Whole Foods

Many whole food nutrients can help not only prevent the onset but also the progression of many degenerative diseases. They can also help you maintain a healthy and active lifestyle. These nutrients can also be found in certain supplements. Take a look at these sources of natural and potent antioxidants such as vitamins A, C, and E as well as the minerals, potassium, and magnesium to fight free radicals that damage our cells. This diet can help protect your body and beauty from long-term damage and disease. Even minerals can help cell metabolism, reduce stress, and improve heart health.

Omega 3, and 6 Fatty Acids Omega 3 (or omega-3 fatty acids) are important nutrients and essential building blocks for the brain and body. They play an important role in building tissues that stay flexible and strong over long periods. They are also essential for the maintenance of healthy eyes, brain, skin, memory, and mood. The sources include organic and non-GMO flaxseed, rapeseed, and walnuts. Salmon oil, tuna, and other cold-water fish sources are also good. These oils can be used in many ways, including the preparation of salads or stir-fries.

Chia seeds and coconut oil can be used as a healthy cooking oil. When used in cooking, it makes food tastier and more nutritious. The oils used should be organic since they are natural and nutrient rich. Organically produced coconut oil contains medium-chain triglycerides that are easier for the body to digest and use for energy. Beef is good because it is high in iron, zinc, phosphorus, and omega 3s which are important for healthy skin, hair, nails, and bone growth.

When it comes to supplements, try to find products that contain a carefully selected amount of natural ingredients, using GMO-free methods. The content can look anything from a natural green or black tea to a slew of vitamins, minerals, and enzymes. Vitamins are particularly helpful in boosting your immune system, as they are easy for the body to absorb and use. Vitamin C, vitamin A, and vitamin D are all important for your skin's protection against free radicals caused by air pollution, sun rays, smoking, and other factors. The skin also eliminates toxins through its pores.

# Chapter 8 Building the Things You Need

Resource conservation and sustainable living are long-standing topics, but the current interest in the field can be traced to concerns relating to global population growth, widespread depletion of resources, and nuclear proliferation. Generally, the term sustainable living refers to subsistence farms that can be sustained in their physical form indefinitely, by the resources harvested from those farms.

To accomplish these goals, people must obtain access to sufficient quantities of quality food, water, shelter, and energy. Regardless of whether living conditions are optimal or suboptimal, one's life circumstances can be substantially improved through proper management of resources and routines. A sustainable living strategy can be manifested in any number of ways, so long as the strategies and actions are taken contribute to the overall goal of sustainability. The strategies listed below are not exhaustive but may provide a useful starting point for people concerned with self-reliance, survival, or sustainability. If these strategies could be implemented on a large scale, people would not have to be as concerned with food, water, shelter, and energy. For example, if food could be stored in vast on-site reserves, people would not have to worry about storing enough food for the next 12 months.

There is no doubt that you are going to need and want some things to help you hold livestock, keep your gardens, and process your foods. Many things can be built yourself, and some can even be made from junk that you already have laying around, or that you can salvage for free or for truly little.

Trade some eggs for what you need with a neighbor. You would be surprised how many people still enjoy a good barter. Bartering was popular long before everyone had money.

Bartering was just as good as cash and we may very well see a time when we rely on this again. He who has the most that can be bartered may indeed be worth more than others.

## The Chicken Coop

A chicken coop needs to be structurally capable of keeping predators out. Don't think that because you live in the city or the suburbs that you don't have wildlife predators, you do. You've perhaps not seen them, but they are there. Foxes, for example, roam downtown Denver at night and coyotes howl in the outskirts of the suburbs, waiting to prowl the shadows after you are in bed. Raccoons are everywhere, as are snakes and possums.

Chicken wire does not make the best wire for a chick coop. Use hardware cloth. It's a heavy gauge and rigid. The holes are too small for a predator like a raccoon to reach through and grab a hen. Even a coyote can reach through a chicken wire fence, and the force with which they will yank your chicken through will break the fence and kill your chickens. Predators will return to easy targets too. Pallets can be found very cheaply if not free in garbage piles. You can pull them apart to use the boards or you can use the entire pallet as a section of wall for anything you like.

With hen houses, you want them to have an indoor coop that is a few feet off the ground, with a ramp they can walk up as they like to roost up high at night. Inside their coop, you'll want to have bedding material and some nesting boxes where they lay their eggs. Build a door that allows you to access the nesting boxes from the outside, which will also make gathering eggs much easier. You will also need an entry door that allows you to clean inside. Change their bedding regularly to keep it clean and fresh.

Inside their yard, give them more than one location for water that is clean and fresh. Waterers for chickens are designed to keep the water clean but you'll need to check it and change it regularly. Inside your coop, add some places for your hens to roost on shelves or 'chicken trees' like a cat perch.

The bottom line is that if you keep the wire with tiny holes, like hardware cloth, snakes and predators cannot access your run. Digging a trench and extending metal sheets or your hardware cloth down into the ground for 12 to 18 inches will ensure that predators who dig (coyotes, fox, raccoons, and possum) can't get into your run when you aren't looking.

A hungry fox will strike during the light of day. Cover your run because chicks and chickens look particularly good to a hawk or an owl. They will swoop down and snatch your birds before you can say 'stop' and it will be too late. Hardware cloth over the top will ensure that nothing gets in. If cost is a factor, an old net from a trampoline works great too. If you can get your hands on the whole trampoline, you can fashion an entire coop.

## Goat Run-In Shelter

Goats don't need a completely enclosed shed and will develop respiratory infections if you keep them in a closed barn. They need a three-sided structure or open building that allows air to always flow through. Give them a roof to hide from the rain and plenty of bedding to flop down in and you'll find your goats happily napping in a structure made with pallet sides and a tin roof. They don't care what it looks like, as long as they can stay dry. Goats don't appreciate getting wet.

A quick run-in shed is something that is one of the easiest things you'll ever put together because you can use the pallets exactly as they are. Use screws to attach them into three walls and lay a sheet of galvanized roofing material over the top and attach it. You're done.

## Garden Fence

For this, you can get highly creative. Any fencing material will do, including things that might not normally be fencing. Make sure that you use something that won't allow small rodents or rabbits in at the bottom. If you have deer in your area, you'll want a fence that is 6 feet tall to keep them out of your garden. One or two deer can devastate your garden overnight, leaving you with nothing to show for all your hard work. Make sure you put something up around your garden and understand that four feet might not be tall enough if you have deer.

You can always add rope around the top, or wire, and string some things on it that will also keep birds away. Tin pie plates work well sometimes. Birds will steal berries, and small vegetables when they are hungry, and they'll often also take your seeds before they've even sprouted.

## A Smoker

This is a wonderful way to preserve meat, especially pork and beef. You can fashion your smoker by scavenging bricks, stones, an old wood-burning stove for parts, etc. It doesn't take a whole lot to build a smokehouse. A wood stove that you can set up outside but run the pipe inside of a shed that you build to hang meats inside of and slowly smoke is a fantastic way to preserve meat for longer and it tastes amazing. Smoked BBQ is some of the best meat on the planet and it's a bit of food art. Those who smoke their meat are picky about the type of wood they smoke because it changes the flavor of the meat.

A little bit of research will show you a hundred different ways that you can fashion a smokehouse from salvaged materials. Add your unique ideas and make it your design. Cement blocks for the base of your building and the woodshed on top of them to smoke your meat in is a simple concept. It's a way of cooking meat that has been used for ages. Some people like to build their smokehouse from cedar. Cedar is a wood that deters bugs and won't rot. It also has a pleasant smell which seems to add to the smokehouse experience.

Inside your smoker, you'll want rods to hang meat on or hooks that can hang from above. The more you can smoke at one time, the more you'll be able to put away and store it at one time. You'll want enough space to smoke a whole goat when you butcher it so that you can process it all at once. One of the quickest and easiest ways to create a smoker is to use an old refrigerator: the older, the better. Place a sheet of metal across the bottom interior of the fridge. Then, place a can of wood chips in the bottom or a small grill that you can load with wood chips. At the top of the fridge, cut three or four holes on each side for vents. Use sheets of hardware cloth for racks and smoke your meat the same day. An old stove will also work as a small smoker. Fish, especially trout or salmon, are wonderful when smoked, so the smoker will get a good workout from your homestead livestock butchering.

# Cold Frames

These will be for keeping your plants and soil warm for several weeks longer than in a typical growing season. They'll also allow you to get plants outside a few weeks earlier than normal. A cold frame can be fashioned from bricks, cinder blocks, or built from lumber and lined with rigid foam board insulation. For the top, a piece of cut Plexiglas will work, framed in a wood frame, or just find an old window that someone is getting rid of. You'll find fifty different ways to use them and could even fashion your greenhouse from them. Cold frames don't have to be permanent but also can be if you've got the perfect spot for them. They should always be in a southward facing position, in the sunlight where they can gain maximum heat. Making your tops removable will allow you to cool them when they are getting overly hot. Adding a screen to the top can turn them into beds that keep moths and bugs away while allowing fresh air and rain.

# Compost Bins

Again, being a fan of pallets, you can fashion a three-section, which entails an open composting container that allows you to just dump into one section, move to the next section when that one is full, and rotate your compost in and out as it is ready. By having more than one section, you'll always have compost that is ready to use.

If you don't want to use pallets, you can use other materials, including old garbage cans, provided that you make sure they can drain and let air circulate. The compost should be moist but not wet. You don't want it to be rained on if you can help it. You also want to allow excess moisture to escape. Another important note is that compost shouldn't stink. If it stinks, it is too wet. It's the moisture that holds the smells in. Composting toilets work on this same dry composting theory.

If you've got cement blocks or bricks, you can also stack them into three-sided structures that you place compost inside of. As an added benefit, place your rain barrels over the top of them to keep the compost from getting too wet and get the bonus of compost that keeps your rainwater warm enough to not freeze in the winter months. Locate your compost bins between your manure gathering stations (chicken coop, goat shed, rabbit hutch) and the garden where you'll be using the compost when finished. This means you'll carry it only as far as necessary.

## Raised Garden Beds

Virtually anything can be recycled into raised bed gardens. Kiddie swimming pools work great. Add some holes for drainage and you're in business. If you want something that looks nice, you can use cement blocks and landscaping stones to make yourself a nice, raised bed without ever driving the first nail. Find a building that has burned and left a mess, as often, owners will allow you to take what you want after they've gotten their insurance check. Look for used materials on Craigslist and don't forget to check the free section. A lot of people have materials that are there for the taking if you are willing to remove them or take something apart to get them. It's shocking what some people will give away for free, frankly. An old boat or canoe can make a wonderful, raised garden bed when the boat no longer holds water. For garden purposes, that's perfect. It also makes it worthless to someone who wants a canoe so you can probably get it for free or unbelievably cheap just to get it out of someone's yard or garage.

Think outside the box to create your whimsical garden or your English garden. It's all in your grasp if you always keep your eyes open.

## Climbing Cages

Some plants need something to climb on. It doesn't have to be tomato cages. Some rope strung back and forth through two pieces of wood, stuck in the ground will work for a lot of plants to climb on. Creating a wood frame from some free pallet wood and then wrapping some rope or wire through the slats can be made to look whimsical and work wonderfully well to support plants. An old ladder missing a bottom rung can be buried into the ground deep enough to stand straight as a support for beans to climb toward the skies or a trellis for ivy, you decide. Just don't let the ladder go to waste. Boards framed into an a-frame with cross slats are a wonderful climbing frame as you can prop two wood pallets together and make this in ten minutes with a drill and some screws.

## Potting Bench

If you are doing container gardens, you will appreciate having a potting bench where you can do your work and have a countertop to use. Old kitchen cabinets can be used, or you can build yourself a nice counter with some 2x4 lumber or pallets. A top can be cut from plywood or using an old door or piece of sheet metal. Shelves, drawers, or storage space for your tools will be a relief to have everything within your reach when you need it. You'll be able to pot faster and easier while saving your back.

## A Simple Hoop House Greenhouse

This is a welcome addition to any garden. You can extend your growing season and protect young plants from rabbits, squirrels, and other problems, such as weather. You'll be able to keep them warmer, out of the damaging winds of summer storms, and the hail that can decimate a garden. All it takes is some PVC, a few rolls of plastic film that can be purchased online or even at a Walmart. You'll need a little lumber, including one long 2x4 that can be used at the top as a ridge board. You'll drill holes the size of your PVC pipe, and slip that through, then secure the PVC into the ground on either side.

You can do this by securing them to 1x4 slats on the ground, using brackets. This adds some weight to the bottom, keeping it from blowing over easily. Those bottom slats can also be secured to stakes that are driven into the ground as anchors to hold it all in place. The ridge board will hold each rib of PVC at equal distances so you can wrap the entire structure in plastic. Frame a door at one or both ends and use any old, scavenged door as your entry.

## Willow Fence

This is an English form of fencing by starting with willow tree limbs, stuck into the ground at an angle. When you've done all your pieces in a row, you can go back to the beginning and weave new pieces across those pieces. You can get highly creative with the pattern and how neatly or wildly you weave your willow cuttings. With luck, those pieces that you've started in the ground will take root and it will begin to grow into a living fence that will keep small creatures out, while providing a natural place for birds to nest. It's a lovely addition to any garden when you need some division between sections or something pretty to look at.

## Cardboard Box Dehydrator

A simple and easy way to dehydrate some of your fruits or veggies using a cardboard box couldn't possibly be simpler, or cheaper. An ideal temperature range for dehydrating is between 125-degrees and 145-degrees Fahrenheit. All you need is a large box, a thermometer, a light fixture for a 100-watt light bulb, and some duct tape.

For the inside of the box, you'll want something that you can use to fashion a rack to dry veggies on. A piece of hardware cloth could work, or a baker's cooling rack will work simply fine. You can prop it on four upside-down cups in each corner or come up with anything that works well for you. You can use tape to secure your box to the counter. Add your rack inside and your lightbulb in the fixture. Drop your thermometer into your rack to hold it in the center and close the box, taping it shut. Give it an hour and check to see what temperature you're at. If it is too hot, use a lower watt bulb, such as a 75-watt bulb. Try again and when you are holding in the perfect range, start with something easy to dry.

Apples, peaches, and cranberries tend to be relatively easy. Layer them on your rack and leave them for about 5 hours and check them. Many fruits can take up to 8 hours. Then, when finished, enjoy your fruits, and use this method as often as you like, saving much of your harvest as dehydrated goodies that can be frozen or stored in jars.

# Chapter 9 Your Backyard Homestead Products

When you are working to provide food in a sustainable manner from your backyard, by following the advice contained herein, you'll be able to provide the majority of your family's necessary food supply. You will have the ingredients to make things that you hadn't thought about before. If you can forage for some additional things, like hazelnuts, you can make your flour in a pinch. Making flour, having eggs, and adding some additions like salt, allow you to make your pasta, pancakes, biscuits, and more.

You've got milk covered, the meat of all types covered, all the vegetables and fruits that you could need. You've learned how to dry your foods, can them, pickle them, ferment them, smoke them, and make jerky of all types. You've even learned how to make a biofuel that can offer you fuel for your generator when power is down, or you need gas in the mower. What else could you possibly need? Soap? You can make that with goat milk. Cleaning supplies? Lemons juiced from your potted lemon tree will cover this and make excellent glass cleaner too.

The point is that if you are creative, you can utilize the by-products from your backyard homestead to create a plethora of items that you'd not even thought about. Many people think that they don't have the time to do all these things, but let's look at it differently.

The use of bamboo for creating sustainable products provides an alternative to harmful deforestation and helps in ensuring a healthy environment. A variety of bamboo products are being used today for making sustainable and eco-friendly products.

Bamboo is used to make many different sustainable building materials. Additionally, natural plant dyes are being used to create eco-friendly clothing that is easily available at an affordable price. The unmissable change in the fashion industry is what has strengthened the objective of sustainable living. There is also a surge in the organic farming industry, in response to the popular demand for sustainable living.

Sustainable living means making use of natural resources in a way that they can be used for sustainable benefit over a long period. Sustainability can be achieved by protecting and preserving the environment. Therefore, I have been slowly replacing as many household items as possible over the last 6 months with reusable or zero waste versions! I was able to do away with a ton of plastic by switching to reusable bamboo makeup remover pads and bamboo drinking straws.

Most people go to jobs to earn money to not just pay bills but to purchase food. Food takes approximately 20% of people's income. Poorer households spend as much as 35% of their income on food while wealthier households spend roughly 8% of their income on food. Most people considering growing their food will fall at the lower end of the income scale and are spending a higher percentage of income on food. Therefore, adding a few extra jobs to the family income can free up a lot of time, allowing for a family to learn to raise food in their backyard with a few extra hours available to spend at home.

The other message here is that creativity is the key when it comes to what you can do for yourself and your family. If you are not starting with a big budget or lots of free time, you can still do much more than you realize with a little thinking outside the box and spending a little bit of extra time to build an additional business or skill.

Homesteading is something that we have all thought about but have not yet acted upon. Whether you are a fresh or experienced homesteader, we all have the same start in our backyard. The benefits that you can derive from the homestead include a decreased impact on the environment, a healthier family, more time to spend at home, and a way to better provide for your family. Enjoy what you can in your backyard and thank you so much for reading this.

## Imagine saving thousands of dollars per year on food.

What could you do with that extra money? Would you pay your house off sooner? Pay off the credit card debt that keeps you awake at night? Pay for your kids' braces in cash perhaps? Let's face it, that is a ton of money and one of the things you could do in time s to work less. Imagine not needing a second parent to work because you've no longer ot to purchase food and cough up a gigantic portion of your income.

he icing on the cake is that there are a hundred ways in which you can earn income rom your homestead. Turn it into a side job that keeps you home, making more than vhen you were schlepping out to a job, spending money on gasoline, or spending hours ach week commuting. You're spending precious time sitting in a car, on the way to a ob that you needed to be able to pay for your car, alongside simply needing a job. What ridiculous circle we find ourselves caught up in!

backyard homestead can help to give you back a lot of your budget, but more than that, t can give you your precious time back. Your time is invaluable, but we trade our time or a weekly paycheck that barely meets the expenses and gives us far less satisfaction han working for ourselves can. In many cases, it takes an extra job to support an off-arm lifestyle, which allows us to lose more precious time.

adly, many people can't afford a homestead right now. It is too expensive to begin one ight now. They are too strapped for cash and they may have a mortgage that won't llow them to generate additional income or even to farm their lot. Remember, savings key to your homestead. You can then, save some money and start your homestead ter on. Slowing down the homesteading dreams is delaying gratification and making ur dreams come true later.

here are a few things that every homestead needs. The first thing that you need is a vell-built storage area. This doesn't have to be anything fancy. A large shed or a small arage will do, but it needs to be able to keep moisture and rodents out. You'll need helving that is sturdy to hold large jugs of white vinegar, food-grade buckets, water arrels, and seed-saving supply bins. You need a cool, dry place to store items such as on-synthetic boots, sweaters, blankets, camping gear, sleeping bags, and tools.

IP: Keep an eye out at yard sales for sturdy shelving. This is a great start to a storage rea. Speaking of storage, many new homesteaders take the old broken dresser from heir kid's rooms and store food in these.

The second thing that every homestead needs is good crops. A new homesteader will get tired of spending money on processed food and it will seem like heaven to know how to grow vegetables from scratch without spending a fortune.

**TIP**: Grow as much of your food as possible. This is a great starter. You could plant a patch of strawberries if you have a greenhouse, and grow herbs such as your basil oregano, mint, parsley, and cilantro.

## Importance of homestead backyard

It is important to have a sustainable homestead if you want to lead a quality lifestyle Use the tips and information provided in this book and improve your knowledge and lifestyle in a few easy steps. You can improve the sustainable homestead by making better choices about the food you buy. Find the best organic meat on the market and purchase it. Be sure you are getting fresh produce from local farms, and you are supporting local growers by adding your money and patronage.

You can improve the homestead by learning new skills that will make your life more fulfilling. Learn how to repair or build new parts for the machines and tools that you own. Customize the items to better suit your needs. Even if the skills are simple, they are ones that can give you more skill and make the homestead more sustainable.

You can make the homestead more sustainable by learning to garden. You can do this by starting your garden or learning to preserve produce from local farmers. Growing vegetables for the family will result in less money spent on food and produce. Develop a productive backyard garden, if you have space as there is no need for the product to get old or rot or go to waste. Your homestead will become more sustainable when you stop throwing away scraps and you start eating the way you used to.

Make your homestead sustainable by learning how to recycle. You should also learn how to avoid anaerobic design and how to be as energy efficient as possible. Instead of paying to pour away water that was used when showers or baths were taken, learn how to put that water to good use. You could use that water for gardening or even cleaning Use your water more wisely and you will immediately reduce your utility bills.

You can make your homestead more sustainable by learning to preserve food. Preserve your fruits and vegetables with fermentation or drying. Make use of your food and turn it into medicine. Eat the food you have grown or preserved rather than throwing it away.

And these methods lead to the greatest sustainable homestead. Begin learning and then do your best to teach others. There is nothing better than sharing your ideas with others and learning from those ideas in return, and that makes for a better homestead, a better you, and a better world.

Therefore, it is important to live in a green and sustainable homestead, because we cannot live in abundance without taking care of our environment. Learn to live as an eco-warrior for the planet. Take note of these tips and apply them to your everyday life!

# Chapter 10 The Benefits of Sustainable Living

Sustainable living is beneficial for both our planet and our society. It is extremely hard to imagine what our world would be if we humans were to continue living in our destructive and unsustainable ways.

## #1. Energy savings:

Environmental science, physics, and evolution all tell us that the sun is the source of all life on Earth. It is only natural that we harness its energy. The survival of our species is very dependent on it, and humans cannot live without energy. The fact is that at the beginning of the 20th century, the world was dependent on fossil fuels for all our energy needs. This is the reason why we currently are looking at global climate change today.

We are now living in the 21st century. While fossil fuels still make up a large chunk of our energy sources, we have now embraced renewable energies like solar energy. It has been proven time and time again that sustainable living is beneficial. With solar energy, our dependency on fossil fuels is slowly diminishing. Our dependency on foreign countries which are essentially politically unstable is also being reduced.

Sustainable living is not only beneficial for the environment, but it is also highly beneficial economically. It is hard to put an accurate economic value on the environment, but we do know that if we were to continue depending on fossil fuels, the amount of money we will spend every year on them is mind-boggling. Solar energy is now a much cheaper solution that poses no harm to the environment unlike, fossil fuels.

## #2. Health benefits:

There are many environmentally safe and healthy alternatives to harmful products. For example, instead of using harmful pesticides and antibiotics, there are organic fertilizers and antibiotics. Sustainable living is not a new concept; it has been around for a long time. It has just been overshadowed by the developed world.

The old renewable ideologies that were used by early civilizations can be used today as well. For instance, organic farming and recycling. The health benefits of sustainable living are quite inexhaustible. For instance, it comes naturally to most people that diesel is safer than fossil fuel, but sustainable living requires us to find alternative fuel options. Sustainable living is probably one of the easiest ways to improve the health of the people in a community.

## #3. Environmentally safe products:

Sustainable living is all about being sustainable. Our governments globally understand this and have developed environmental legislation that is keeping us on track. It is important to focus on the long term to give your home a high grade, long-term investment. One of the easiest ways to create environmentally safe products is by finding and using environmentally safe building materials.

## #4. Common sense and efficiency:

One of the easiest ways to find environmentally safe building materials is to go online and research them. Where else could you go but the internet? Other ways of finding environmentally safe building materials would be in the stone and timber stores or from landfills. The sustainable building often requires a little more effort, but the payoff is huge in many ways. You must think about your future by sacrificing a little now. It is a lot shorter to sacrifice a little now than to regret it in the future.

## #5. The future:

It is believed by many that sustainable living is beneficial for the future. It works because every little thing we do right now will benefit those to come. We are handing them a safe and sustainable future. It is time to get rid of our old ideologies for something new and unique for the new generation. Traditional building materials were more for utility than functionality. Also, most of the materials used were not durable.

Luckily, this is not the case today. Sustainable living is now a high priority when it comes to the building of any structure.

## #6. Helping someone:

Regardless of whether you are going green for the environment or saving money, it is important to understand that sustainable living will help not only the environment or society you live in, but also the lives of other people. It is better to wake up tomorrow and know that we have left a better world to come. How long is sustainable living on humanity's to-do list? Sharing knowledge with others is a good way to ensure sustainable living. If you are an architect, then help your clients choose better materials that will last longer than others. It is for the future of humanity, and it is your responsibility to make it a better world for the generations to come whether they live in your home or elsewhere.

The future of our building materials and our way of building is in the past. In the past, our ancestors were environmentally aware. They were only using sustainable resources and were wise builders because they knew that their structures would be used for quite some time. As modern professionals, we must look for ways to improve the old builds.

## #7. Caring for the environment:

Our generation needs to listen to our ancestors and to add our new modern knowledge to their old methods. It is our job to grow and learn from our mistakes, and to make things better for the future. Caring about the environment is something that people should be applauding us for. It is something that the long-term generations should be commended for, instead of ridiculing us for consuming and polluting. It is not something that we deserve for just destroying everything. It is not others' responsibility to bail us out for creating the mess in the first place.

## #8. Protecting our world:

We must protect our world firsthand. It is our job to protect what's ours and following sustainable building techniques is the first step towards that. Sustainable living is all about protecting something from being destroyed in the future. Not often does a person hink about how hard it was to acquire those resources that we conveniently use every day? It is hard to understand exactly how important it is to never become wasteful. The problem is that this kind of stuff is overlooked and often taken for granted. Whichever way you look at it; sustainable living is slowly becoming a necessity for all generations.

## 9. High priorities for teachers:

Everyone is a teacher of something. As students, we learned certain methods of building and a certain way to build something. We watch other people and take in their knowledge. These methods could be different but are still required around the world. As professionals, we are taught certain things that we can use in certain positions and what is expected of us to do. These are things that are required for a profession, so it can be expected that we carry on with it. We build our lives and how we live of making life better for the future. What is expected of us is to be of a certain standard.

## 10. Gaining knowledge:

Gaining knowledge and finding sustainable living ideas is different for everyone. It is different for children and adults. For some, it is more fun to create stuff than to learn how. For others, the reverse is true. However, what is important is that we find ways to manage with our new but old knowledge. It is great to see how people with different personalities learn things. Therefore, they can see how others deal with the same ideas and use their solutions for their life. They can continue to learn how to live. Sustainable living is a constantly evolving process. It is not something that we keep watching from far.

## 11. Appreciation:

A sustainable lifestyle can help people understand how important it is to appreciate everything. We should learn and appreciate everything that we do. Our actions are not just some small idea that only affects ourselves, but its effects might reach further than what we can ever imagine. Yes, our actions might be small, but it affects a lot of people. It allows us to see what we can do, and we should share those values with others. What will we value in the future? Will it be what we value as a society? It is up to us to do what we think is right.

## #12. Realistic knowledge:

One of the most important things when learning about sustainable living is that it is realistic. The smartest generation that's going to be created in the future is also going to be the most knowledgeable. We should use our knowledge and our sources to find something that is going to be a solution. Instead of building everything with up-to-date methods, we should be creative and find solutions that may work for the future. We need not stick to the ways that we have been taught, but to find ways to improve them and follow realistic concepts. Sustainable living is realistic.

## #13. Creating a future:

As seasoned professionals, we must find ways to build the future. We need to teach our future generations about how to be environmentally conscious as we know how. We should not focus on the things that we cannot teach them, but rather focus on the things we understand about today's reality. Our future generations have a lot more to learn than just the things that we know. They need to learn about how we should learn.

In the future, our learning methods should be booming with creativity. What we learn in school should be creative and interesting. It should be something that a person can relate to themselves, as well as within their own life. The world is still young. It is still growing and developing and improving. What we learn now should lay the foundation for the future. It should lay a foundation for a better economy, for a better species.

Sustainability is essential to our future as a species, and we need to find a way to sustain our future. We must find a way to make this sustainable! It falls upon our shoulders as people, as a nation, and even as a young species in a cosmic cycle of life to find a way to sustain the future. Sustainability is our responsibility. It is our collective responsibility as a society. And each of us, each one of us, has the power to change our little bits of the world. We have the power to make it a little bit better. We have the power to stabilize and improve the future of our species.

Everybody is interested in zero waste living. We all want to be more sustainable. But what exactly does it mean to go zero waste? Well, zero waste means that you don't trash things. Anything that you bring into your life doesn't come with trash. That's a grand idea. It means zero trash. To be more specific, it means traveling zero waste. That means no plastic. I will try to be as specific as possible, but zero waste is a science-based term.

What is zero waste? You're trying to dispose of things in the best way, you're trying to consume the things you use in the best way possible. It's about living a life that does not produce trash. And it's based on the three R's: reduce, reuse, recycle. We can reduce what we use, we can reuse things, and then we can of course recycle it, which can be split into different forms such as by composting. Therefore, it's important to have a composting facility like a backyard compost pile. That's why you need to pick up all your trash. It is especially important for the future. We must take care of what we use so that it does not end up in a landfill.

Now, the only problem is if you want to have a zero-waste life, you're going to need to sort of separate your trash from your recycling and your reusable products. When you go to the grocery store, you need to distinguish between the two. You need to purchase items that are entitled to recycling versus items that are not entitled to recycling. You're allowed to use recycled items in general. But you can't just toss the recycling and the trash into the trash can.

This is also a good time to remind everybody that plastic bags are not recyclable. They get placed in the recycling and they land in the landfill along with all the other plastic trash. They're not recyclable. When we toss plastic bags into the trash, it is equivalent to throwing away an entire plastic water bottle.

The whole point of going zero waste is reducing and getting rid of the trash. The intention is to try and be more eco-conscious, to make a difference. Once you've figured out this magic system of zero waste, then you can just put it into practice. It starts with a little bit of effort to learn how not to generate trash and to instead, help the environment. You can start by making sure that you do not put plastic bags in the recycling bin but recycle everything else. You can grow a compost pile to upcycle or at least break down most of your waste in the yard. You can use cloth shopping bags instead of plastic bags. There are so many ways to replace plastic bags.

The odd thing is most people who teach "zero waste" are not happy that they must teach this concept. There's a little bit of trauma because you must show people why they can't use plastic bags at all. You must teach them about the packaging in the grocery store, and why it's not eco-friendly to throw away plastic bags that you buy in the store. You must show them how you get rid of the plastic by replacing them. And, if you're not going to use one, it's a little bit traumatic, at first. Sometimes the people who teach you zero waste, don't like to do this either. But it's important not to let anyone else off the hook about what their choices are. It's their choice to make an effort to go zero waste. It's your choice to do this too. It's your choice to make an effort.

Without being negative, we choose to go zero waste, and it starts with a little bit of effort. There are some negative aspects around the concept of throwing away plastic. It comes down to a cultural thing. We have so many social enforcement messages such as, do not litter, use only recyclable materials, you must do it etc. etc. But it is valid to set a more elevated goal. It's not just doing whatever you want. It is about making the conscious lifestyle choice to do something better.

It's a little bit of effort to get started, as there's a little bit of work that needs to be done, but you can do it to make a difference. You can contribute to the planet in such a way that you're not adding another plastic item. There are so many things that you can do to easily save tons of waste. For starters, you can create less trash. It's not just about being zero waste. It's about just being a little bit more eco-conscious. Start where you can. Start with a little bit of effort.

To start on your path to zero waste, you must recycle everything of value. The recycling bin is the ultimate starter to go zero waste. That's the first step. You can't just put a bunch of trash in the bin. You can't just throw away a bunch of garbage. That's not zero waste. But recycling plastic and metal are so easy now. The red, white, or black recycling bin in your hallway is a huge start in the system. That's your first step. You don't have to change anything about your whole house if you don't want to. Maybe you don't want to change anything about your whole house. Go ahead and do it incrementally, one thing at a time. That's a good way to start your journey if it's your first time.

First, you must get the recycling or garbage on your property in the red bin. This involves a bit of infrastructure such as a recycling system. If you have waste, you don't have a zero-waste system. You must cut down on your waste, first. Zero waste is quite simple. It doesn't have to be a lot of work. If you ever get overwhelmed, the best way to help you get to zero waste is to put things back. Sometimes it's hard to save all that stuff but throwing it away is not zero waste. Putting it in recycling is your best way. It's not a hard thing to do. You can use old plastic in your garden. What we're doing in this book is that we're using them to create gardens that take care of the earth. We're lowering our plastic consumption and helping the earth.

You must think in terms of global change and environmental conservation. Going zero waste is big. There are some ways to cut down on your waste but consider the bigger picture. You must rethink your entire daily life. You must ask yourself a little bit more about your choices and your home choices. You must think of the eco-conscious choice.

# Conclusion

I hope that this book has given you the tools you need and some extra motivation to start you on your zero-waste home and sustainable living journey. It's no easy feat and it's a change that you make slowly over time. Pick a few key areas to work on first and when you are comfortable take on a few more. Even though it takes every fiber of your being to change your habits let me stress, it is worth it. You will feel better physically and emotionally. You will be saving money without even thinking about it. You will be putting your money towards things that enrich your life rather than send it down the recycling bin. You will be conserving our resources and doing your part to fight climate change. Your life will be enhanced by the joy of zero waste living.

A few things to remember throughout the process:

1. Zero waste living is a slow process. It is not something that you rush into overnight. Take it slow and steady and at your pace.

2. A waste audit is the key to successful sustainable living.

3. Learn to say no to unnecessary plastics and disposable items. God gave us hands for a reason.

4. No guilt! You should not feel guilty for the things you don't do or feel bad for buying things in paper or plastic packaging. Realize that every step counts (even if it's back to square one).

5. Prepare your family ahead of time when introducing changes to a zero-waste lifestyle. It may take some time for them to get comfortable with the new changes you make. Sometimes they are helping you with your zero-waste journey, but other times they're not thinking about the impact of their choices. Find ways to work with them.

Education and awareness are the first steps towards a smooth transition to a sustainable life. Everyone will have to make sacrifices, but because it is better for our planet, it's

etter for future generations and us. Hope that everyone will be a responsible citizen
nd follow suit for a sustainable future.

he most important thing is to DO SOMETHING TODAY! Start with small changes and
xpand as you feel more confident.

ONGRATULATIONS! You have broken loose from the chains of consumerism. You
ave found yourself. Your sustainable living has begun.

Iow, live a happy sustainable independence.

# Note from the author

Thank you so much for reading my book. I really hope you enjoyed it.

Before you go, I have one small favor to ask. Would you mind going to Amazon and writing a review for this book? I'm on a mission to help others learn about sustainable living and the simple steps they can make that will make a great difference, and every review I receive helps this book climb the charts and reach new readers. With enough reviews, we can impact many people, and work together to save our planet!

I read all my reviews and take them very seriously. I also use them to make updates to this book and get ideas for future projects.

Every little bit helps.

Thank you again!

Dominica

Printed in Great Britain
by Amazon